WRITING WITH LOGIC IN MIND

WRITING WITH LOGIC IN MIND

Robert Boyd
Texas Christian University

Harcourt Brace College Publishers

Fort Worth Philadelphia San Diego New York Orlando Austin San Antonio
Toronto Montreal London Sydney Tokyo

Address editorial correspondence to:
Harcourt Brace College Publishers
301 Commerce Street, Suite 3700
Fort Worth, TX 76102

Address orders to:
Harcourt Brace & Company
6277 Sea Harbor Drive
Orlando, FL 32887
1-800-782-4479 outside Florida
1-800-433-0001 inside Florida

Printed in the United States of America

ISBN: 0-15-501909-0

4 5 6 7 8 9 0 1 2 3 066 9 8 7 6 5 4 3 2 1

To
Brian and Amanda

WRITING WITH LOGIC IN MIND

Table of Contents

Preface

Writing depends upon logic. Normally when we write, we have a point to make, and we try to support that point. Supporting a point depends on logic. This work book should help the student make the connection between writing and elementary logic. WRITING WITH LOGIC IN MIND is not intended as a comprehensive work for either writing or logic.

This work book was designed so that a student can accomplish the ten assignments with minimal special instruction. Any assignments that an instructor wants to grade from this work book can easily be detached. {Requiring students to submit the major assignments found on pages 2, 9, 15, 21, 43, and 47 is recommended.} This work book should aid instructors who teach Introduction to Philosophy, Introduction to Logic or most courses across the curriculum where writing arguments is involved. Because it is brief, it can be used in any course which involves writing. However, this work book does have its limitations. It is not intended to address all of the problems involved in writing, nor does it present all acceptable formats for writing. The emphasis of this work is the logic required for good writing, not writing itself.

Two important features of this work: 1) it is student oriented and 2) it presents inductive logic as an important form of reasoning used in writing. Students provide their own text to critique.

A special thanks must be extended to Dr. Neil Daniel (Texas Christian University) and two of his students, Diana Breclaw and David Wells, for providing me with numerous suggestions. Also I wish to publicly thank Ms. Barbara Johnson, the Director of the Writing Center at Tarrant County Junior College - Northwest Campus, for her encouagement and advice. For many reasons I want to thank my colleagues in the Philosophy Department at Texas Christian University. Not only are they colleagues from whom I have learned much, but they are friends. Leanne Winkler, Editorial Assistant for Harcourt Brace, must be thanked for providing recommendations and guidance in preparing this work for publication. As always I am indebted to my family for allowing me to pursue my impossible dream.

Exercise I

Introductory Project

In the space provided on the next page write a brief essay supporting either the pro-life position or the pro-choice position concerning abortion.*
The position you support is not crucial. The essay will become the basis for the remaining exercises and will be revisited in each.
While you could definitely write more in support of your position, limit your essay to the provided space. Make sure that you think before your write - plan your essay.
*** Grading of this exercise will be based upon whether the assignment is finished as assigned. ***

*For alternative writing prompts, check the suggested list at the end of the workbook.

Name: ____________________ Section: ____________

Exercise II

Arguments

While you may not have thought about it, writing involves the use of arguments. You have been told that each time you write you should have a main point, i.e., a thesis. Then the body of your work should contain information that supports the main point. While there are times when we write simply to describe a situation, most writing involves the presentation of evidence for a given claim. Roughly speaking, that is an argument. An argument consists of making a claim and supporting that claim. The study of arguments enables us to write more concisely and persuasively and gives us a better understanding of writing. It aids in the presentation of claims and their evidence, and helps these presentations conform to acceptable standards of rationality.

Notice how each of the following brief passages contains a claim and support for that claim. These are examples of simple arguments.

II.1

```
If salt is mixed with water, then the salt will
dissolve.  This pan has water in it, so if I put
salt in it, the salt will dissolve.
```

II.2

```
Sulfuric acid when mixed with water creates a
violent reaction, consequently one must take
care when mixing acids with water.
```

II.3

```
Winners concentrate on winning, but losers
concentrate on getting by.  One is either a
winner or a loser, but not both.  Coach Sullivan
is a winnner for he does not concentrate on just
getting by.
```

II.4

```
Union threats are no news.  Therefore, union
threats are good news, since no news is good news.
```

In the first example, the claim is "if I put salt in the pan of water, then the salt will dissolve." The evidence or the support for this claim is presented in two pieces. The first is, "If salt is mixed with water, then the salt will dissolve." The second piece of evidence concerns the pan in question having water in it. What is the claim in II.2; in II.3; II.4? What evidence is being cited in each example as support for the claims you just identified?

An argument will always contain a claim, better known as a **conclusion**, and supporting evidence, known as **premise(s)**. If a passage fails to contain either of these elements then it is not an argument. The following examples are passages that do not contain arguments.

II.5

If it rains, then I will take my umbrella.

II.6

Every single person is a self-made person, but only the successful admit it.

II.7

Don't forget your umbrella!

II.8

Did your essay involve an argument?

These examples do not constitute arguments by themselves; however, they may be used as part of an argument. For example, conditional statements (II.5) are not considered to be arguments, but they may be part of an argument, as in example II.1. What kind of sentences are examples II.6 - II.8? Notice that such passages do not contain a thesis and support for that thesis.

Writers often make use of indicator words that aid in the identification of the various parts of an argument. Words that typically point out the evidence are known as **premise indicators**. Claims are often highlighted by **conclusion indicator** words. The following lists include some of the more common words.

Premise Indicators

Because	Given that
For	Since

Conclusion Indicators

Consequently	So
Hence	Therefore

Look at examples II.1 through II.4. Circle the indicator words used in those arguments. When you wrote your essay, did you use any such words? If so, circle them.

Just as there are different kinds of instruments in a band, there are different kinds of arguments. Two types of arguments are basically good, and we will learn to write arguments modeled after examples of each. However, one type of argument is to be avoided when writing. This type is known as a **fallacy** and will be discussed more thoroughly in several of the following exercises.

Basically a fallacy is an argument that violates some standard for correct reasoning.

Some of these violations are easily determined. Examine examples II.1 through II.4. Which is fallacious?

The other two types of arguments are **deductive** and **inductive** arguments. There is much misunderstanding concerning the difference between these argument types. Ever since Aristotle (the Father of Logic, 368 - 335 B.C.), a misconception has been taught concerning the difference between deduction and induction. The misconception is that an argument that moves from general information (e.g., "most swans") to a conclusion about a particular (e.g., "the third swan") is a deductive argument. In inductive arguments, it has been claimed, the evidence is concerned with particulars and the conclusion is a generalized claim. As we will see later, this way of distinguishing between induction and deduction will not always work.

A deductive argument has the following characteristics:

1. The conclusion is claimed to be true assuming the premises are true.
2. The premises provide conclusive evidence for maintaining the conclusion.
3. The conclusion does not deal with any information which is not present in the premises.

An inductive argument has the following characteristics:

1. The conclusion is not claimed to be absolutely true, based on the premises.
2. While the premises provide support for the conclusion, its support is not conclusive.
3. The conclusion does deal with information that is not found in the premises.

Inductive arguments tend to expand our knowledge, whereas deductive arguments do not. Inductive arguments are generally evaluated in terms of their content. Deductive arguments are evaluated according to their structure or form. Again, look at II.1 through II.4. Which argument is such that if its premises are true, then the conclusion must also be true? That is, which argument is deductive in nature? Which argument is such that even if its premises are true, its conclusion might be false? This last question will help identify the inductive argument.

If you identified II.4 as the fallacious argument, you were correct. II.1 and II.3 are deductive in nature, and II.2 is inductive.

There is one last misconception concerning the difference between induction and deduction. It is easy to fall into a habit of thinking which elevates deductive reasoning and takes a dim view of induction. Both types of reasoning are legitimate and equally important. It is improper to place an emphasis on one to the exclusion of the other. A good writer will need to use both types of reasoning.

Whether you are evaluating someone else's argument or writing an argument yourself, it is important to properly "see" the line of reasoning which is taking place in an argument. Seeing the line of reasoning is enhanced by rewriting the argument into **standard form**. Standard form is simply the listing of the premise(s) above a solid line. Below that line, the conclusion is listed. For example, II.1 would be rewritten as follows:

II.9

```
If salt is mixed with water, then the salt will dissolve.
This pan has water in it.
__________________________________________________________
∴  If I put salt in the pan, the salt will dissolve.
```

The (∴) is used to stand for 'therefore.' Notice that by putting the argument into standard form, the reasoning presented by the argument is clearly seen.

Reread your essay from exercise 1 and identify any arguments you presented. In the space below clearly state your position and list each piece of evidence supporting your position. Then write your argument in standard form and try to determine whether you intended it to be inductive or deductive. Notice the following example.

II.10

```
Position: John should attend Shelby State and not Northwest.
    1.    Students find course credits from Shelby State are
           easily transfered, but Northwest students find it
           difficult to transfer credit.
    2.    Graduates of Shelby State are in demand and I do not
           know anything about Northwest students' job
           prospectives.
    3.    Shelby State has offered John a scholarship; Northwest
           has no scholarships to offer.
    4.    Shelby State offers a greater number of majors when
           compared to Northwest.

          Transfer of credit
          Job potentials
          Scholarship
          Number of majors
          ----------------------------------------
          ∴    John should attend Shelby State
```

Ask a classmate to read your original essay, looking specifically for your argument. Did they identify all of the premises you intended to present?

Your essay concerning abortion, or the assigned topic, should have been a series of premises since the assignment was to defend a position. Did you clearly state the position you wanted to defend? In defending your position did you also provide support for the claims which you used as evidence for the major conclusion? Did you state why the line of reasoning was relevant to the issue? As a writer, you want your reader to follow your line of thinking. Make sure the main points of your reasoning are clear. As you rewrote the arguments above, did you have to search for them or were they obvious? Finally, seldom are we really prepared to present an argument on the spur of a moment. Typically it is **essential** that we do a little research on the topic. The claim we want to support will only be as strong as the evidence cited in its support.

In the space below rewrite your essay making the overall argument clearly seen. Be sure to include why the evidence cited is relevant to the position you are defending. Again, the key is not which position you have defended, but how you defend it. Also keep in mind that usually when a piece of writing is evaluated quality is much more important than quantity.

Name: ______________ (B) Section: ______________

Exercise III

Writing with Clarity and Relevance

When we read an argument written by someone else, we require two basic features of that argument. First of all, the argument must be written such that it is understandable. That is, the reasoning should be **clear** and not misleading. Furthermore, we require that the evidence be **relevant** to the claim of the conclusion. We have all seen advertisments claiming that a particular group drinks Coors Lite. This particular group of young people is extremely good looking and is having a fabulous time. The implication the beer producers want you to draw is that if you drink their product, you will look like that group and will have just as much fun. Few of us really accept the evidence as being relevant to the implied conclusion.

Just as we expect someone else's argument to have clarity and relevance, the arguments we write should have the same desired features. Often this is difficult, because "it's perfectly clear to me!" occurs frequently in the writing process. In this exercise we will briefly examine some common ways each of the desired features are violated. These are often identified as fallacies.

A fallacy is a violation of some standard of correct reasoning.

There are four main pitfalls to be aware of that lead to ambiguity or lack of clarity when writing arguments. The first occurs when an improper emphasis is placed on a given word or phrase. This is called the **fallacy of accent**. While this fallacy normally occurs when we are quoting someone else, it also can occur in our own arguments. When it occurs in an argument, an improper claim is drawn by putting an unwarranted emphasis on a given word or phrase.

III.1

It has been claimed that "to really live you must freely give." Since you are not freely giving, we should have your funeral because you are not really living and if you are not living you must be dead.

The above argument is placing an improper emphasis upon the word "really."

A second common error in writing arguments leading to a violation of clarity is known as an **amphiboly**. An amphiboly occurs when improper syntax or grammar is used and results in an ambiguity of meaning. That is, because of the error, the argument could be interpreted in more than one way when in fact only one interpretation is accurate. This often happens with homonyms.

III.2

> John told me that he was going to stop at the costume store to pick up his suit of mail for the masquerade party tonight. He must be going as a postage stamp.

The fallacy of **equivocation** is the result of a third common mistake that leads to lack of clarity in an argument. As with an amphiboly, an equivocation involves a sloppy use of words. Whereas in the amphiboly only one meaning is accurate, an equivocation uses the same word or phrase but gives different meanings each time it is used.

III.3

> Man is an inventor. No woman is a man. Therefore, no woman is an inventor.

Clarity can also be violated in an argument when the audience to whom the argument is addressed is not taken into consideration. If the audience is a group of non-math majoring college freshmen, then a mathematical proof supporting Heisenberg's program would probably lack clarity. The point here is, when writing an argument, take your audience into account. Use words and examples that your audience will clearly understand. If your argument requires the use of unfamiliar materials, you need to educate your audience. After all, when you are writing an argument, you are trying to convince someone else that your position is correct. If they cannot follow your argument, they are not going to accept your conclusion. (Or at least they shouldn't!)

The second feature all good arguments must have is a relevancy between premise and conclusion. Violation of this feature leads to the group of fallacies known as fallacies of irrelevancy. Some of the more common members of this family are:

Fallacy of Appealing to Force
Fallacy of Appealing to the People
Fallacy of Appealing to Pity
Fallacy of Abusiveness
Accidental Fallacy
Argument from Ignorance
Fallacy of Begging the Question
Fallacy of a Complex Question
Fallacy of Composition
Fallacy of Division
Irrelevant Conclusion

Of these fallacies, four are extremely common for the novice argument writer.

> Have you ever noticed how most people like to do things that everyone else is doing? People like to go to Disney World because everyone else is going. But you, the individualist, don't want to be like everyone else. You don't want to be like those other people. Because of this, you should buy our car. It shows your individualism.

The above argument is an example of the fallacy of **appealing to the people**, also known as the Bandwagon Effect. Remember those arguments you ***used to*** present to your parents. "But Mom - Everyone else is going to ______________!" While there are times when what others do/think is relevant - it is not always the case. Any argument which is dependent solely on that type of thinking is flawed.

A second common error in writing arguments is the fallacy of **abusiveness**. We have a tendency to become verbally abusive with our opponents. Consider the issue of abortion (your essay). Have you ever heard:

A pro-lifer say:

> Concerning my opponent - She is just a baby killer!

A pro-choicer say:

> Concerning my opponent - He is just out to steal our rights!

When you are arguing for a position, slander should never be a part of your line of reasoning - even if what is said is accurate. Avoid making statements that are likely to harm the reputation of a person.

For the student just beginning to develop their critical reasoning skills, the fallacy of a **complex question** is a common pitfall. This fallacy occurs when a complex issue is dealt with in a rather simplistic fashion. That is, a very complex issue is handled as if there was one and only one viable position. Consider the abortion issue again - it is a very complex issue, but how many times has it been approached as if there was only one legitimate side? This does not mean that positions cannot be taken. What it does mean is that you must acknowledge alternative positions.

You should show the strengths of your opponents' position. You should point out the weaknesses of your own position. Then you must show why your position is the best alternative in spite of its weaknesses and the opponents' strengths.

Finally, the fallacy of **irrelevant conclusions** is another one to look out for. To avoid this fallacy simply make sure you ask yourself if the conclusion is really relevant to the premises you have cited. If you recognize that not everyone will see the connection, you should tell your reader how it is connected. It is your responsibility as a writer to provide the bridge or assumptions that connect the evidence offered to the claim of the conclusion.

Revisit your latest version of the essay. Did you violate either clarity or relevancy? Rewrite your essay making sure that your argument has the proper clarity and relevance.

Name: ______________ (C) Section: ____________

Exercise IV

Guiding Your Reader

Read the following paragraphs. {The assignment was to write a brief paragraph either supporting or refuting the practice of capital punishment.}

IV.1

Concerning the issue of capital punishment, I must agree that it is a difficult problem. I have a very hard time accepting the fact that capital punishment results in the death of another human being. I just can't condone killing anyone. However, I realize that some crimes might be so bad that not to punish the criminal is like endorsing the crime. After all the victim also has rights. Consider the individual who would walk onto an elementary school campus and just start shooting and killing innocent kids. If anyone deserves capital punishment, surely that type of individual does. However, the Bible somewhere says, "He who has done no wrong, let him decide the judgement."

IV.2

While the issue of capital punishment is a difficult problem, I am against it. In order to declare a person's crime is worthy of capital punishment, they must first be found guilty of a particular crime. How can we as human beings sit in judgment of another individual. We are all sinners. All of us have made mistakes. It seems to me that, just as in every day life, we should always learn from our mistakes. If we support capital punishment, the criminal is not allowed to learn from his mistakes. Just think of the horrible mistake we might make of finding a person guilty of a crime, then executing him, only to discover that he was innocent. If we reject capital punishment, such serious mistakes could never happen. For these reasons I am opposed to capital punishment.

IV.3

> The issue of capital punishment will always be controversial. However, I do believe that capital punishment is an appropriate type of punishment for some crimes. I support the death penalty for the following reasons. First of all, in the case of certain crimes the only punishment which defends the sanctity of life is the death penalty. Secondly, it is society as a whole which pays when we incarcerate a criminal for life. A third reason for supporting capital punishment is the message it sends to prospective criminals. If you play, you pay. Now I realize that some reject the death penalty because of the potential of executing the wrong person. That is, an innocent person might be put to death. However, as Dr. James, an expert in the area who happens to reject capital punishment, has pointed out, this objection does not have much support. Historically, according to Dr. James, it has not been a problem. He even acknowledges that this argument against the death penalty is a straw man. For these reasons and others, I support capital punishment.

Whether or not you agree with the position taken in each paragraph, how would you evaluate their effectiveness? Was the position taken by the writer clear to you as a reader? Did the paragraph take a stance, as required by the assigment? Was the line of reasoning easy to follow?

> Remember, as a writer who wants to be understood, it is your responsibility to take the reader by the hand and lead them down the path you choose. Whether they agree with your argument is their responsibility, but it is yours to make sure they can follow your argument.

If your goal is to make your reader walk in your shoes, then you should make sure your writing contains three distinct parts. Depending on the length of your writing, these individual parts may occur in a single sentence or in a series of chapters. You must have:

> **1) A clear and distinct opening**
> **2) A coherent and consistent body**
> **3) A concise closing**

In the opening section of your work you should clearly state what is to take place in the remainder of your work. If you are taking a stance, then the position you are taking should clearly be spelled out. Notice in essay IV.1 the writer fails to clearly take a stance. Compare and contrast the opening statements found in each of the above essays. Which opening statements do you find most successful and why?

The body of any piece of writing should contain evidence supporting the position taken. That information should not conflict and it must be relevant to the issue. The body should be written in a way that, it clearly reflects the line of reasoning being used. Notice that in essay IV.2 it is difficult to clearly "see" just what is being offered as evidence. It is difficult to distinguish one point from another. Contrast this with IV.3. The three major points of support are clearly identified. Again, whether a reader agrees with the line of reasoning is not the issue. At issue is whether the reader can follow the line of reasoning desired by the writer. Besides using the numerical expressions, i.e., "first," "second," the reader can be guided by the use of <u>transitional words</u>. Just as premise and conclusion indicator words direct the reader, transitional words also provide direction.

Some key transitional words:

Furthermore	**But**
Then	**Next**
In addition	**However**

Notice that some of these terms indicate additional points, i.e., along the same vein of thinking as the previous point, whereas others indicate contrasting points.

The closing part of your writing should capture the entire work. The closing section may contain a brief statement of the entire argument, or if the work is brief, it may only be a restatement of the position taken.

The third essay includes an important element often omitted from works which intend to support a given position. It contains an acknowledgement of a supporting point for the opposing position. Not only does it present an opposing line of evidence, it briefly deals with that point. A good position paper should acknowledge weaknesses in the position taken, and deal with those weaknesses. Since no issue of real significance is clearly one sided, these additional elements are important. These two additional elements tend to portray a sense of fairness and open-mindedness on behalf of the writer. If a reader finds a work totally one sided, then an attitude of skepticism often develops from the audience.

Re-examine your essay as rewritten on page 15.

Did you clearly take a stance?
Have you made use of transitional words to guide your reader?
Have you acknowledged weaknesses with your own position?
Did you acknowledge a strength in your opponents' position?

Rewrite your essay. (Additional research may be required.)

Name: ____________________ (D) Section: ______________

Exercise V

Inductive Arguments I

The purpose of this exercise is to introduce you to two major forms of inductive reasoning. The first form will be that of an Inductive Generalization and the second will be that of a Simple Enumeration.

Reminder: Inductive arguments do not intend to guarantee the truthfulness of the conclusion based on the evidence offered.

An inductive argument has the following characteristics:

1. The conclusion does not claim to be absolutely true, based on the premises.
2. While the premises provide support for the conclusion, its support is not conclusive.
3. The conclusion does deal with information that is not found in the premises.

Inductive Generalizations

The basic characteristic of an inductive generalization is that it uses particular instances as evidence of support for a claim which is general in nature.

V.1

Swan A is white
Swan B is white
Swan C is white
∴ Most swans are white

V.2

John received an A in Creative Writing, as did Peter, Joan, and Mary. We can conclude that all of the students received an A in that course.

When writing inductive generalizations, there are two specific criteria that must not be violated and by which the relative strength of the argument is evaluated. **Sample size**, or the number of instances cited as evidence, and **sample diversity**, or diversity among the items listed, must be taken into consideration. When evaluating sample size or sample diversity, the writer should take into consideration the scope of the conclusion. If the conclusion is a claim about all students in a given course, then the number of students listed as evidence should be proportionate to the total number of students in the course. Unlike deductive arguments, inductive arguments have relative strength. For example, let's say that the course had 15 students in it. Clearly 13 or 14 students cited as evidence would be more than adequate. Furthermore, 1 or 2 would be clearly inadequate. But what about 4, or 5, or 10?

Inductive arguments are evaluated as 'strong,' 'moderate,' or 'weak,' depending on their relative strength.

The problem is further accented when we realize that one individual may believe that the sample size is adequate whereas another may find it questionable. If either criterion is violated, the argument is automatically considered to be weak, it is fallacious. If sample size is violated, the fallacy committed is known as a **hasty generalization**. If sample diversity is violated, then we have the fallacy of **biased statistics**.

All fallacious arguments are weak arguments, but not all weak arguments are fallacious.

Re-examine V.2: Is its sample size adequate? What about the sample diversity? As a reader of that argument, I would have to raise questions concerning both criteria. Since the author of that argument has failed to provide me with crucial information, I probably would not evaluate it as a very good argument. (Since I don't know if either criterion is violated, I could not say it is fallacious.) This illustrates the importance of providing sufficient information when using inductive generalizations in order for the argument to be properly evaluated.

Another important point when writing any inductive argument is the relative strength of the conclusion.

One way to make an inductive argument stronger is to weaken the claim. Instead of claiming that 'all students received an A,' change the claim to 'many ' or 'most.'

In this exercise rewrite part of your argument concerning abortion, or the assigned topic, such that the evidence you list deals with particular instances and the conclusion is a generalization. (It may take several attempts before you have written a good inductive generalization.)

Simple Enumeration

This type of inductive argument moves from evidence that is particular in nature to a conclusion that is also particular.

V.3

```
Swan A is white
Swan B is white
Swan C is white
∴ Swan D is white
```

V.4

```
John received an A in Creative Writing, as
did Peter, Joan, and Mary.  We can conclude
that Mandie also received an A in Creative
Writing.
```

The relevant criteria for simple enumerations are **sample diversity** and **total evidence**. Total evidence requires that no pertinent information is withheld which might alter the conclusion. For example, in the case of V.3, let us assume that the author of that argument knows that swan D is an Austrian swan. But since he wants to claim a particular point, he withholds that information. As a result, our evaluation of the argument would be changed because Austrian swans are typically black. Hence, given this assumption, the criteria are violated and the argument would be an example of the fallacy of **incomplete evidence**. As an author, you should never intentionally withhold information which would alter the assessment of an argument. As a reader, when you are confronted with simple enumerations, you must always examine the evidence and question whether information is being withheld.

Now rewrite part of your argument concerning abortion, or the assigned topic, such that it is a simple enumeration.

___

___

___

___

___

Exercise VI

Inductive Arguments II

In this exercise we will continue our study of enumerative arguments. The two kinds of enumerative arguments to be developed here are Arguments from Analogy and Statistical Syllogisms. In the second exercise we learned that it is inaccurate to characterize induction as arguments that move from premises which are particular in nature to a conclusion that is a generalization. In the last exercise you may have noticed that inductive generalizations did have that characteristic, but simple enumerations did not. Neither of the argument types in this exercise follow the stereotype. In fact, you will notice that statistical syllogisms follow the pattern of the stereotype for deductive arguments.

Arguments from Analogy

VI.1

```
Swan A is white and lives in the FTW Zoo
Swan B is white and lives in the FTW Zoo
Swan C is white and lives in the FTW Zoo
Swan D lives in the FTW Zoo
________________________________________
∴ Swan D is possibly white also
```

VI.2

```
John took Creative Writing and received an A
Joan, Beth, and Kathy all took Creative Writing
and all received A's
Brian also took Creative Writing
________________________________________
∴ Brian probably received an A
```

The argument from analogy moves from statements about particular items to a claim about another particular item. Unlike simple enumerations, the subject of the conclusion is introduced in the premises. The line of reasoning is dependent upon the analogy that is presented. This argument type has but one criterion to satisfy -- **relevancy of the analogy**. However, this criterion does have two aspects. In evaluating arguments from analogy, a critical thinker must examine both the relevant similarities and the relevant dissimilarities between the items being compared. If the analogy fails, we have a fallacy of **false analogy**.

Develop an argument from analogy supporting your view. (Beware - good arguments from analogy are difficult to write.)

Statistical Syllogisms

VI.3

```
98% of all the swans in the world are white
The FTW Zoo just acquired a new swan
∴ The new swan is white
```

VI.4

```
Most of the 20 students in Professor Albright's
Creative Writing class received A's.  From this
we can conclude that Joe, who was in that class,
possibly received an A.
```

Statistical syllogisms are evaluated by **sample size** and **total evidence**. The higher the percentage, the greater the likelihood that the conclusion is accurate. In VI.3, if the percentage had been 75%, then the argument would be considered weaker than it is at 98%. (That does not mean that the argument is weak, it is only weaker.) How strong of an inductive argument would it be if it had been 100%?

The question is a trick question, for if it had been 100%, it would not have been an inductive argument. For if the premises were true, then the conclusion would have to be true. It would have been a deductive argument. So as you write statistical syllogisms, you want the sample size to be as close as possible to 100% without attaining it.

In the last exercise it was mentioned that the stronger the claim, the weaker the argument. Notice the claim in VI.3; "The new swan is white." This conclusion is not claiming that the swan might be white based on the information provided, but that it is white. This claim is extremely strong and very difficult to support in an inductive argument. Therefore, this argument would be weaker than you might have suspected given the 98% sample size.

The assignment is to write an argument in the form of a statistical syllogism that supports your position concerning pro-choice or pro-life.

____

____

____

____

Exercise VII

Deductive Arguments I

In this exercise we will deal with those deductive arguments known as Conditional Arguments. However, we need to briefly review the basic nature of deductive arguments.

A deductive argument has the following characteristics:

1. The conclusion is claimed to be true assuming the premises are true.
2. The premises provide conclusive evidence for maintaining the conclusion.
3. The conclusion does not deal with any information which is not present in the premises.

An interesting question is "how can deductive arguments guarantee the truthfulness of the conclusion assuming the premises are all true?" Good deductive arguments are designed or structured such that if the premises are true, then the conclusion must be true. Whereas inductive arguments are evaluated according to their content, deductive arguments are evaluated according to their form. If they have an acceptable form or structure, they are called valid. If they have an unacceptable form, they are invalid. When writing deductive arguments we always want to write valid arguments.

Conditional arguments may appear in two valid forms. The first is known as Affirming the Antecedent because one of the premises affirms the antecedent of the other premise which is a conditional statement, i.e., If ..., then .... In this argument type the conclusion will simply be a restatement or affirmation of the consequent.

VII.1

```
If swan A is white, then swan B is white
Swan A is white
∴   Swan B is white
```

This is a valid argument form because if the premises are true, then the conclusion must be true.

The second valid form of conditional arguments is known as Denying the Consequent. As the name implies, in this form the one premise states a denial of the consequent found in the other premise. In this case the conclusion will be a denial of the antecedent.

VII.2

```
If swan A is white, then swan B is white
Swan B is not white
∴  Swan A is not white
```

Examine each of the following examples and determine whether they are affirming the antecedent or denying the consequent. Write your answer on the provided line.

VII.3

```
If the truck does not start, I will stay at home
I did not stay at home
∴  The truck did start
```

____

VII.4

```
If the truck does not start, I will not get home
I did get home
∴  The truck did start
```

____

VII.5

```
If the truck does not start, then I will stay at home
The truck did not start
∴  I stayed at home
```

____

VII.6

```
If the truck does start, then I will not stay home
The truck did start
∴  I did not stay at home
```

____

{Examples VII.3 and VII.4 are Denying the Consequent, and VII.5 and VII.6 are Affirming the Antecedent.}

Two argument forms that are similar, but invalid forms, are denying the antecedent and affirming the consequent. These are invalid because it is possible for the premises to be true and yet the conclusion to be false. Since these forms are invalid, you will always want to avoid writing arguments in these forms.

VII.7

```
If it is raining, then I will get wet
It is not raining
∴   I will not get wet
```

VII.8

```
If it is raining, then I will get wet
I am wet
∴   It is raining
```

The easiest way to write conditional statements is to use the standard 'if ..., then ...' form as the examples above illustrate. However, we can express the conditional statement by various means in English.

In the following sets of statements, each of the statements of that set is considered equivalent. Thus, they can be used interchangably.

If it rains, then I will get wet.
Whenever it rains, I will get wet.
Given that it rains, I will get wet.
It rains only if I get wet.
A necessary condition of it raining is my getting wet.

If it rains, then I will get wet.
I will get wet if it rains.
I will get wet since it rained.
I will get wet so long as it rains.
A sufficient condition of my getting wet is that it rains.

Write six valid conditional arguments supporting your position on abortion, or the assigned topic. In at least two of them use alternative sentence forms instead of the standard 'if ..., then ...'

Exercise VIII

Deductive Arguments II

In addition to the conditional argument forms, valid arguments may be written in other acceptable forms.

VIII.1

Joan attended the party
Mary attended the party
∴ Joan and Mary attended the party

VIII.2

Joan and Mary attended the party
∴ Joan attended the party

VIII.3

Joan and Mary attended the party
∴ Mary attended the party

VIII.4

If Joan goes to the party, then Mary will go.
If Mary goes, then Peter will attend
∴ If Joan goes to the party, then Peter will attend

VIII.5

Joan will go to the party
∴ Joan will go to the party or Mary will

VIII.6

Joan will go or Mary will go to the party
Joan will not go to the party
∴ Mary will go to the party

VIII.7

```
Joan will go or Mary will go to the party
Mary will not go to the party
∴ Joan will go to the party
```

Write four valid arguments which reflect four different argument patterns. Again, these arguments should deal with your position on abortion, or the assigned topic.

Just as we saw that conditional statements could be written in various acceptable forms, certain other sentence forms have acceptable alternatives. (Some of these alternatives, while logically correct, are not generally accepted forms of good writing.)

It is not the case that John and Mary passed.
John did not pass or Mary did not pass.
John and Mary did not pass.

It is not the case that John passed or Mary passed.
John did not pass and Mary did not pass.
Neither John nor Mary passed.

If John passes, then Mary will pass.
John does not pass or Mary passes.

If John passes, then Mary will pass.
If Mary does not pass, then John did not pass.

Re-examine your argument and develop a brief valid argument supporting your position.

Exercise IX

Being Fair-Minded

One additional element from logic will be acquired to enhance your writing abilities.

A good writer must be fair-minded. Just as it was stressed earlier that a good writer must take a stance and not ride the fence, a good writer must be fair with the opposing position.

One of the best ways to learn an opposing position is to develop an argument that supports that position. If this argument is as strong as possible, then you have a good understanding of your opponent's position, and as a result a better understanding of your own.

Learn to walk in your opponent's shoes.

In this exercise you are to write an argument supporting the <u>opposite</u> position you took in the earlier essays. (This will probably require additional research.)

Your grade for this exercise will be based on your logic, use of transitional words, avoidance of ambiguity and irrelevance, and your fairmindedness and objectivity.

The purpose of this assignment is not to change your position, but to help you better understand the other side.

Name: ____________________ (E) Section: ________________

Exercise X

Putting It All Together

In this exercise you will rewrite your position making use of both deductive and inductive reasoning.

Be sure to avoid violating clarity or relevancy.

Guide your reader by using transitional words.

Helpful hint: Try following the steps below.

1. In an earlier exercise you developed a deductive argument to support your position. Use that argument as your outline.

2. Make your deductive argument provide the structure for your main argument.

3. Each premise of that deductive argument can be supported by means of inductive reasoning. That is, develop an inductive argument to support the premises of your deductive argument. Each premise of your main argument will be a conclusion to an inductive argument.

4. This will result in a series of paragraphs with each containing an inductive argument. The main points of each paragraph when put together will form a valid deductive argument.

Name: ______________________ (F) Section: ________________

ALTERNATIVE PROMPTS:

1) Protection of jobs versus Protection of environment
2) Should the purchase of handguns be controlled?
3) Is capital punishment justified?
4) Should television programs be censored?
5) Should textbooks be censored?
6) Is it right to use undercover cops on school campuses?
7) Should we make condoms available in public schools?
8) Is economic isolationism correct for America?
9) Should hunting as a sport be allowed?
10) Is it right to spend the big dollars on sports programs when academic programs are being cut in our schools?
11) Should college atheletes be paid?
12) Should we send financial aid to foreign counties?
13) Do we need a national health care program?
14) Is the No-Pass, No-Play rule fair?
15) Should we seriously consider making our public schools move to a twelve month calendar?
16) Should prayer in schools be banned?
17) Columbus: A hero or a villan?
18) Should the Supreme Court Justices serve life terms?
19) Should our public schools adopt school uniforms for all students?
20) Is inter-racial marriage right?
21) In a pluralistic society, is it better to have no religious preference or to allow the majority opinion to rule?
22) Should we down-scale the military?
23) Are standardized tests fair?
24) Should we allow students to graduate with Spanish as their only language?
25) Should we have a separation of church and state?
26) Is recycling worth it?
27) Should children be allowed to divorce their parents?
28) Should corporal punishment, within reason and guidelines, be allowed in our public schools?
29) Are we violating an individual's rights by banning smoking in some areas?
30) Has our lawsuit mentality gone too far?
31) Is euthanasia justifiable?
32) Are professional athletes paid too much?
33) Should girls play high school football?
34) Have we gone too far with EEO and AA policies?
35) Is it ever right to break the law in order to promote some higher goal?
35) Do businesses really have an ethical responsibility to their employees?
36) Do animals have rights like humans?
37) Should private clubs/organizations have the right to selective membership?
38) Should the U.S. have an "open door" immigration policy?
39) Should we limit the number of terms a person can hold a congressional office?
40) Should gays be allowed in the military?
41) Does agent free will entail that the agent could have done otherwise?
42) Is discrimination on the job ever permissible?
43) Does urine screening by employers or prospective employers violate the right to privacy?

44) Does the concept of 'greatest possible being' entail the notion of existence?
45) Are dress codes in our public schools appropriate, even if they may violate someone's cultural beliefs?
46) Is an act good if and only if it conforms to some law or standard?
47) Should drugs be legalized?
48) Should the United States provide aid to other countries like Bosnia or Kuwait when our own people are homeless, jobless, and hungry?
49) Is it fair to give preferential treatment to job applicants based solely on race to fill quota?
50) Should the current grading system be revised?
51) In our public schools, should we be emphasizing safe-sex or abstinence?
52) Does the First Ammendment give the media the right to invade an individual's privacy?
53) Is the purpose of a history text to simply tell the facts or to interprete the facts?
54) Should the parole system in our state be totally abolished?
55) Should one person's freedom of speech be allowed to violate someone else's freedom of privacy?
56) Should animals be used in experimental lab testing?
57) Do homeowners have the right to use deadly force when protecting material items?
58) Should taxpayers provide daycare facilities for teen-age mothers still in school?
59) Is there truth in advertising?
60) Should minors who are convicted of serious crimes be treated as adults?
61) Should automobile companies be penalized for not developing more energy efficient vehicles?
62) Is the role of the news media to merely present the news or should they provide commentary on the news?
63) Do metal detectors in public buildings protect or violate an individual's rights?
64) Do schools have the right to ban certain books from their libraries and classrooms?
65) Should some music be censored?
66) Is school busing a good way to deal with segregation?
67) Should schools have the right to dictate what courses a student must take in order to graduate?
68) If you were in a position to implement any policy, what policy would you enact to improve race relations? (Defend your choice)
69) Should centers of higher education be ran simply as another big business?
70) Should homosexual lifestyles to taught in public schools?
71) Has the media ignored the rights of the accused by broadcasting information not yet ruled as admissible in a court of law?
72) Should the tenure system adopted by most colleges and universities be abolished?
73) Are there any universal truths?
74) Does 5+7 necessarily equal 12?
75) What value do lobbies perform in our political system?
76) Should we abandon the electoral college system used in our presidential elections?